Whose Baby BUTT?

by Stan Tekiela

Adventure Publications
Cambridge, Minnesota

Dedication

To my darling daughter, Abby.

Photos by Stan Tekiela
Edited by Sandy Livoti
Cover and book design by Jonathan Norberg

10 9 8 7 6 5 4 3 2 1

This may just look like a brown and round butt . . .

. . . but when this critter grows, you'll need to look up.

Whose baby butt is this?

It's a baby Moose!

Moose have short tails that are hard to see. Baby moose are tiny enough to walk under their mother's belly without ducking. **WOW!** When they grow up, their legs become more than twice as long as the legs of White-tailed Deer. Adult moose can step across fallen logs with their very long legs and wade across streams without getting their bellies wet.

The fur isn't enough to stay totally warm on this butt . . .

. . . but the tail acts like a blanket that keeps this animal cozy when sleeping.

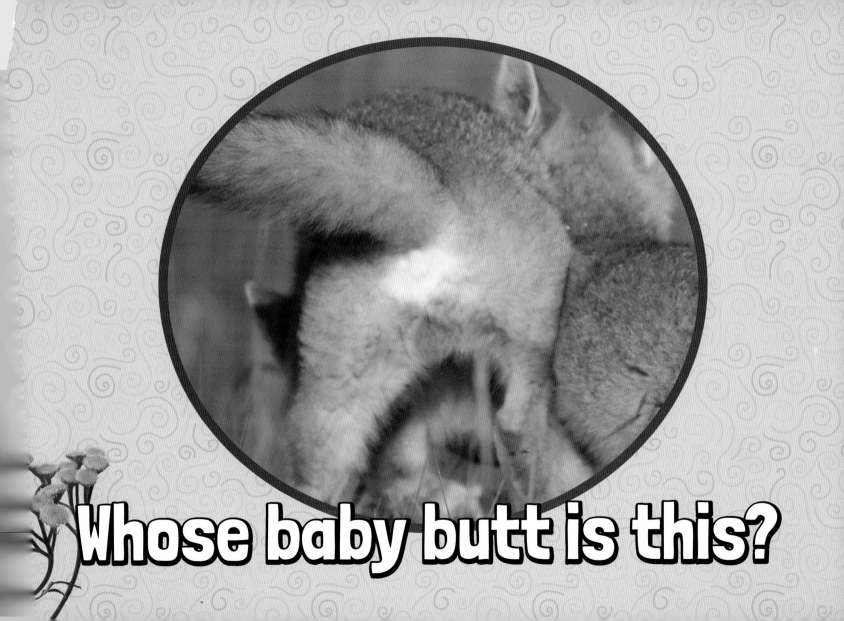

Whose baby butt is this?

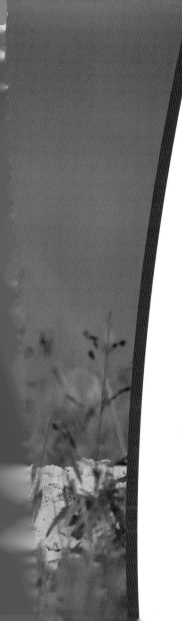

It's a baby Fox!

The swift fox is one of the smallest foxes in the world. Mommy and Daddy weigh only four to five pounds—about half the size of a small dog. This makes the foxes super fast. **VAROOM!** Swift foxes live in underground burrows. When the parents are out hunting, the pups chase each other and play with their leftovers from last night's dinner.

The tail is short, round
and fluffy-like-cotton
on this butt . . .

. . . but it's not a cotton ball.

Whose baby butt is this?

Rabbit!

The eastern cottontail is the most common rabbit in the United States. It is named for its cotton-like tail. **CUTE!** Bunnies are born in a nest lined with their mother's fur, which keeps them warm. Once they leave the nest, they eat flowers and grass. Their ears get even longer as they grow up.

Tan and tiny compared with the parents' butts . . .

. . but you won't confuse this fluffy bird with any other.

Whose baby butt is this?

It's a baby Crane!

Sandhill cranes are some of the tallest birds in America, but their hatchlings are teeny tiny. Cranes have two babies each year. Baby cranes are called colts, just like baby horses. And just like horses after birth, cranes walk right after hatching. They follow their parents everywhere. Sometimes they walk several miles a day. **PHEW!**

There's a pink, wiggly and naked tail at the end of this butt . . .

. . . but it's not a worm.

Whose baby butt is this?

It's a baby
Opossum!

Virginia opossum babies are cute with their tiny, funny-looking tails. These tails act like an extra-special hand. **HANG ON!** Baby opossums can hang by their tails, but as they grow, they become too heavy for upside-down fun. As opossums get older, they use their tails to grip and balance while climbing in trees.

This baby has a white
and woolly small butt . . .

. . . but it's not a baby sheep.

Whose baby butt is this?

It's a baby
Mountain Goat!

Baby mountain goats bounce around the rocky mountaintops where they live—almost like they have springs in their hooves! The dizzying heights don't seem to bother them. **OH, MY!** When the mothers are feeding, the babies like to play king of the hill.

Fuzzy and cute, this
is not a bare butt . . .

. . . but all of this fur helps
protect this creature.

Whose baby butt is this?

It's a baby
Bear!

Brown bears are not always brown . . . **WHAT?** They can be tan, reddish, or even pure white. Their thick fur is very important. It keeps them warm, protects them from bug bites and shields their skin from the sun.

See the short, fuzzy tail with a black tip on this adorable butt . . .

. . . but look quick before it zips into a burrow.

Whose baby butt is this?

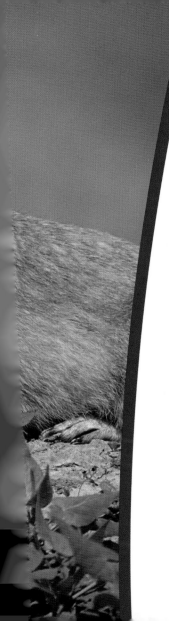

It's a baby
Prairie Dog!

Black-tailed prairie dogs live in large families with lots of brothers and sisters—as many as eight pups. Sometimes one will play with another's tail or bite it. **OUCH!** It's all part of the fun and games in a prairie dog town. Aunts, uncles and cousins live nearby, and everyone visits for some good times.

This long, rough tail can be on a farm animal's butt . . .

. . . but you can see it here, or there, or just about anywhere.

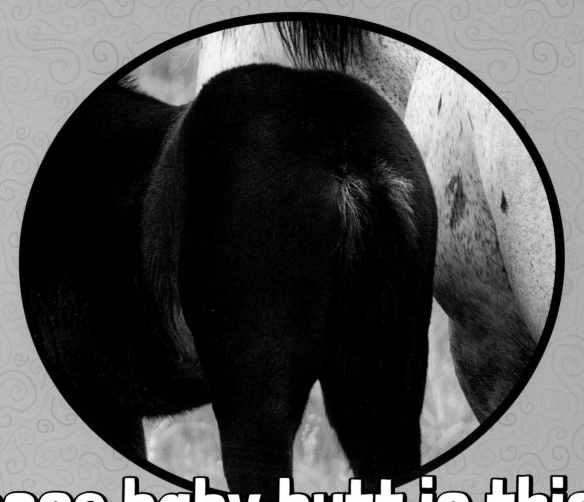

Whose baby butt is this?

It's a baby
Horse!

Wild horses still roam in America. A colt is a young boy horse. A filly is a young girl horse. A foal is a boy or girl horse, usually under one year of age. Wild horses can run super fast, reaching 25 to 30 miles per hour. **ZOOM!**

More fuzzy than feathery, this baby has a tiny wet butt . . .

. . . but there's a good reason why it's wet.

Whose baby butt is this?

It's a baby
Loon!

When common loons hatch, they're covered with brown fuzz that looks like hair. It's actually feathers. Loons spend most of their lives in water, so they're always wet. But water rolls right off their butts. Baby loons can swim underwater right after hatching. **SPLASH!** Mom and Dad feed them tiny fish.

Animal Facts

Moose

Baby moose (calves) walk within one to two hours of birth. Even though they are tiny when born, they grow up to be the tallest land mammals in North America. Males (bulls) can be 7½ feet at the shoulders—even taller with head and antlers. Each antler can weigh 30 pounds or more. Females (cows) are shorter and lack antlers. Moose are able to swivel each of their ears separately to hear what's ahead, behind and on both sides, all at the same time.

Swift Fox

Deep in underground dens, swift fox babies (kits) are born tiny and helpless with their eyes closed. Their parents are bigger but only about the size of a house cat. They make their homes in shortgrass prairies in western states. Swift foxes became nearly extinct by the 1930s due to a control program that sought to eliminate all predators. To save the species, they were reintroduced to many places in their former range.

Eastern Cottontail

Cottontail mothers have three to four litters per year. Each litter has up to seven baby bunnies. Bunnies are in the nest for about two weeks before heading out into the world. If you see a baby cottontail that's fully furred and has its eyes open, no matter how small it looks, the bunny is on its own. Cottontail rabbits eat green vegetation during spring, summer and fall, and switch to woody plants in winter. They forage for food mostly at dusk and dawn, resting during the daytime.

Sandhill Crane

Sandhill crane parents build a mound nest with aquatic vegetation, and the mother lays two eggs. Tiny babies hatch after 28 to 30 days and grow quickly. Adult cranes have the longest trachea of all birds, giving them the ability to make some of the loudest calls. You can hear them trumpeting up to a mile away. Baby cranes don't call. Sandhill cranes are named after the Sandhill region in Nebraska. Fossilized crane bones have been found in Nebraska dating back 10 million years.

Virginia Opossum

The Virginia opossum is North America's only marsupial. Marsupial babies develop in a fur-lined pouch on the mother's belly. After leaving the pouch, babies ride on their mother's back, holding tightly onto her fur. By the time they're large enough to walk on their own, the mother has very thin fur. Opossums are true omnivores and will eat just about anything they can find. They have more teeth than any other land mammal in North America. Opossums are expanding their range across the country into northern states and the Rocky Mountains.

Animal Facts (continued)

Mountain Goat

Baby mountain goats (kids) can walk within minutes of birth. After a couple days they are able to scamper around on the rocks and play with the other kids. When they are all grown up, both the males (billies) and the females (nannies) have long, beard-like fur on their chins. Mountain goats aren't related to other goats. They live in high-altitude habitats, usually in elevations above 13,000 feet. Their thick, shaggy white coats keep them super warm in winter.

Brown Bear

Baby brown bears (cubs) are born in an underground den in midwinter, weighing only one to three pounds. They are just a tiny fraction of the size of their mother. Cuddling with the mother keeps them warm, and the diet of mother's milk keeps them growing fast. They don't leave their den until the warm spring weather arrives. Brown bears are the most common and widespread bear species in the world. They live in forests and open tundra in northern North America, Europe and Asia.

Black-tailed Prairie Dog

Prairie dogs are highly social, burrowing critters that live in tightly knit family units. They dig complex underground burrow systems, complete with separate rooms for food storage and bathrooms. Outside, they stand on a mound at the entrance to watch for predators approaching their colony. Prairie dogs bark to communicate, and they have an extensive variety of sounds. Special barks alert others when danger is near. One indicates a land predator, while another warns of an aerial threat. They might have the most complex "language" of animals in America.

Wild Horse

Horses arrived in North America with the Spanish explorers in the 1500s, and some escaped into the wild. Today, their wild descendants inhabit many western states. Baby horses are birthed in spring and are able to walk and follow their mother within just minutes of birth. The babies are born with the colors, spots, stripes, patches and patterns they will have their entire life. Wild horses are also known as mustangs. The name "mustang" comes from the Spanish word *mustengo* and means "ownerless beast."

Common Loon

Common loons lay only two eggs each nesting season. Babies ride on their parents' backs during their first 10 to 11 days. After that, they're too large to climb aboard, and they swim alongside the adults. Common loons live in freshwater lakes in northern states during summer and in salty ocean water during winter. They are some of the only birds that can switch back and forth between freshwater and saltwater environments. During winter they excrete the excess salt they take in through special ports near the base of the bill.